# The Adventures of Sinbad the Sailor

# Monkeys and Monsters

Written by Rosalind Kerven
Illustrated by Evelyn Duverne

Ahoy there, you lazy little jellyfish! Do you like adventures? Well, my name's Sinbad the Sailor and I've come to tell you about *my* amazing adventures, out on the salty sea.

Monsters ... pirates ... villains ... I've seen them all!

Come on, sit down on this barrel. Make yourself comfortable and I'll begin.

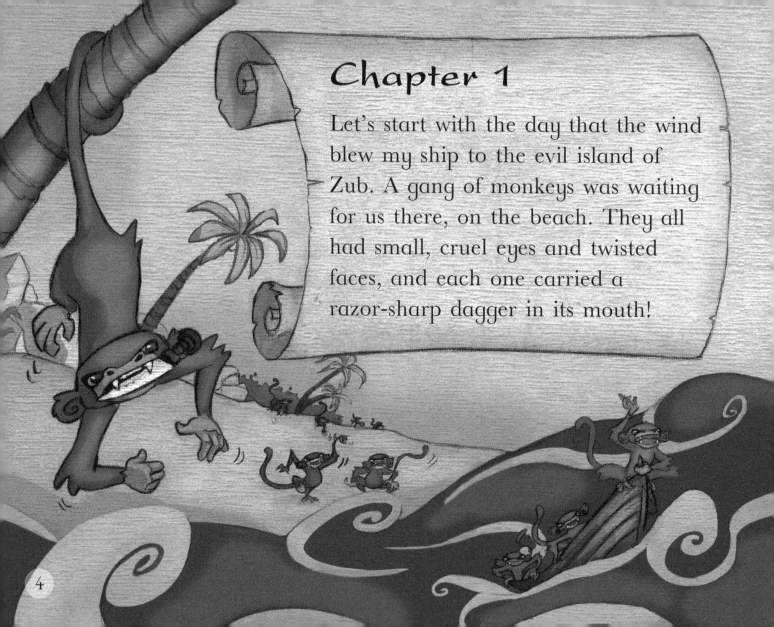

# Chapter 1

Let's start with the day that the wind blew my ship to the evil island of Zub. A gang of monkeys was waiting for us there, on the beach. They all had small, cruel eyes and twisted faces, and each one carried a razor-sharp dagger in its mouth!

"Help," screamed the captain.
"They're coming to get us!"

Sure enough, the monkeys came swarming onto the ship, seized everyone on board – and tossed us all into the sea!

As we thrashed about helplessly in the waves, the monkeys grabbed the oars, turned the ship and sped away in it.

Somehow, a few of us managed to swim ashore. But now that the monkeys had stolen the ship, we were completely stranded.

You should have heard the other passengers groaning and moaning! But I was determined not to give up. So I gazed around the island … and very soon spotted a towering castle.

"Let's go up there," I said to the others. "The gates are wide open. Someone inside might help us."

We all trudged through the gates into a dark courtyard. There was no one around. An enormous bonfire was blazing away in the middle of the yard, with a blackened cauldron steaming on top of it.

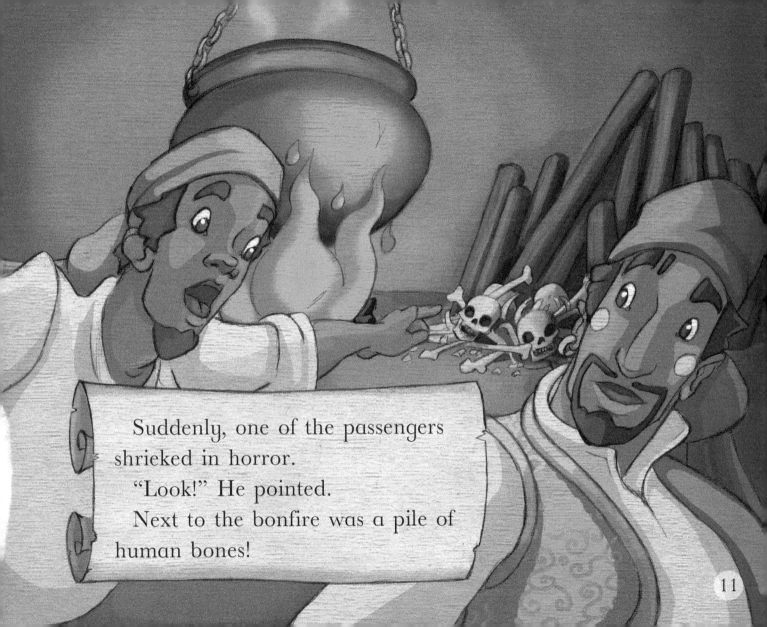

Suddenly, one of the passengers shrieked in horror.

"Look!" He pointed.

Next to the bonfire was a pile of human bones!

# Chapter 2

As we gazed at the bones, we heard heavy footsteps behind us. We spun round – just as a fearsome ogre came stomping into the courtyard!

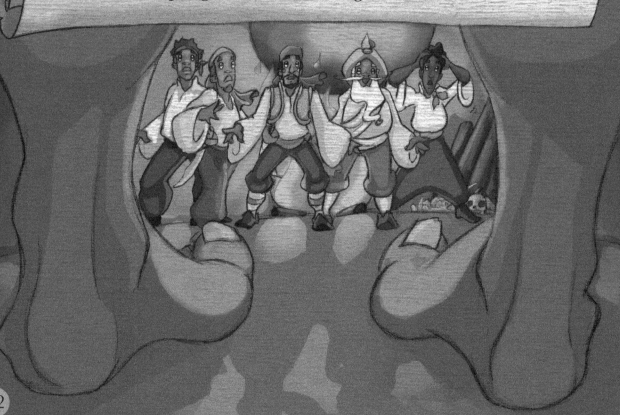

He was as tall as a tree and as fat as an elephant. Blood was trickling out of his broken, blackened teeth.

He crouched down and began to sniff us, one by one, with his great hairy snout.

13

We all drew our swords and waved them bravely.

The ogre bellowed with laughter and jabbed at us with a filthy finger. Then he snatched up the captain and hurled him into the cooking pot!

The rest of us watched helplessly as the ogre stirred the captain round the cauldron with a gigantic spoon, licking his lips with a greasy, scabby tongue.

"Quickly," I hissed to the others. "He's too busy to bother with the rest of us. Here's our chance to escape!"

# Chapter 3

While the ogre prepared his gruesome meal, we grabbed some logs from his bonfire. We found some rope and tied the logs together to make a raft.

Dragging the raft behind us, we crept out of the castle and ran back to the beach. We launched the raft into the sea and the tide began to carry us away. But just then ...

... the ogre came striding down the beach!

"COME BACK, YOU SLIPPERY WORMS!" he roared.

"Faster, faster!" I urged my companions. We all paddled frantically with our hands.

The ogre began pelting us with rocks from the beach. It was terrible. There was nowhere to hide.

One by one, he knocked my companions into the sea, and every one of them was drowned.

But I was lucky.

I escaped and drifted on the raft all by myself for countless days and nights, through thunderstorms, whirlpools and crimson sunsets. At last, I was washed up on the shores of another island.

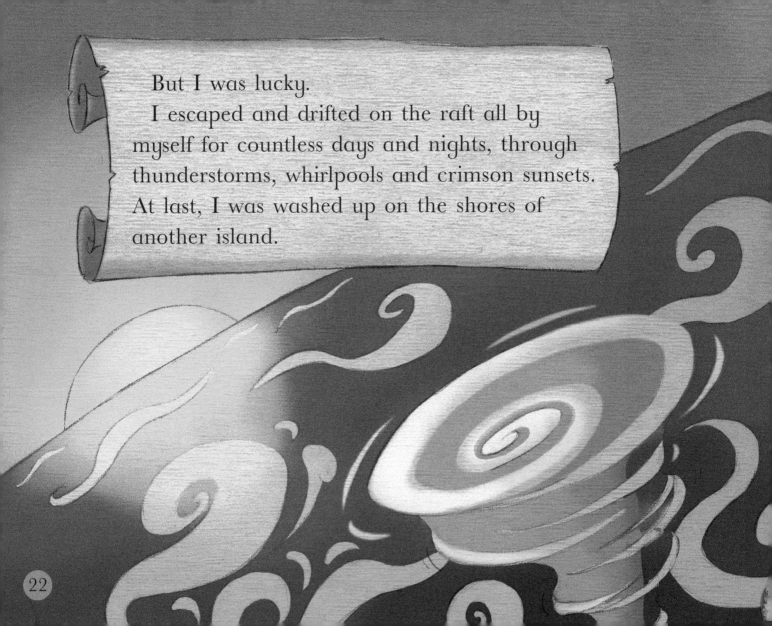

This island was covered in a lush forest, and all the trees were laden with delicious fruit. Soon, I was stuffing great handfuls of figs, dates and bananas into my mouth. Wonderful!

Feeling much better, I set out through the trees to explore.

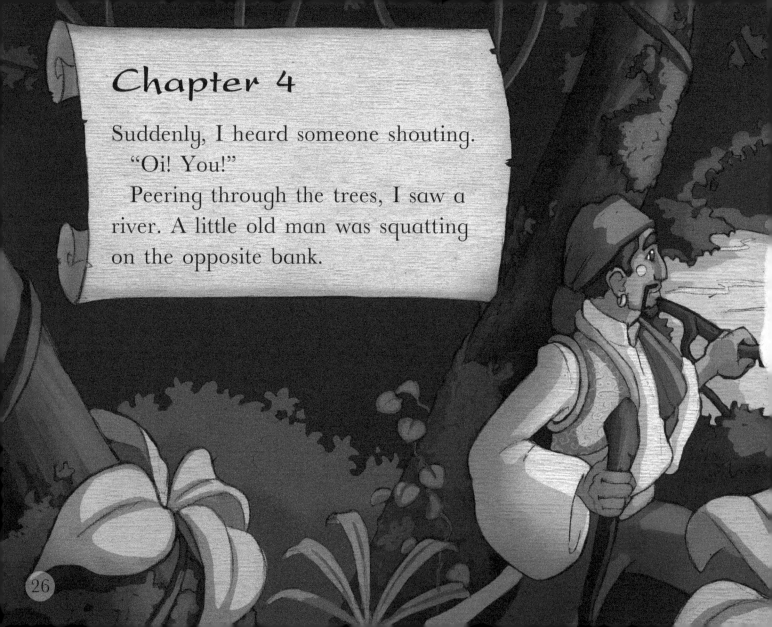

# Chapter 4

Suddenly, I heard someone shouting.

"Oi! You!"

Peering through the trees, I saw a river. A little old man was squatting on the opposite bank.

"Help!" he whimpered. "I can't get across!"

"Don't worry," I called back to him. "I'll come and get you."

I waded into the water and lifted the little man onto my back. But he didn't say "thank you". Instead, he started kicking, punching and scratching me.

I tried to shake him off, but he clung to me even tighter, like a limpet on a rock.

"I'm staying on your shoulders for ever!" he cackled. "I'm the Old Man of the Sea. Ha-ha! Hee-hee! You've just become my slave!"

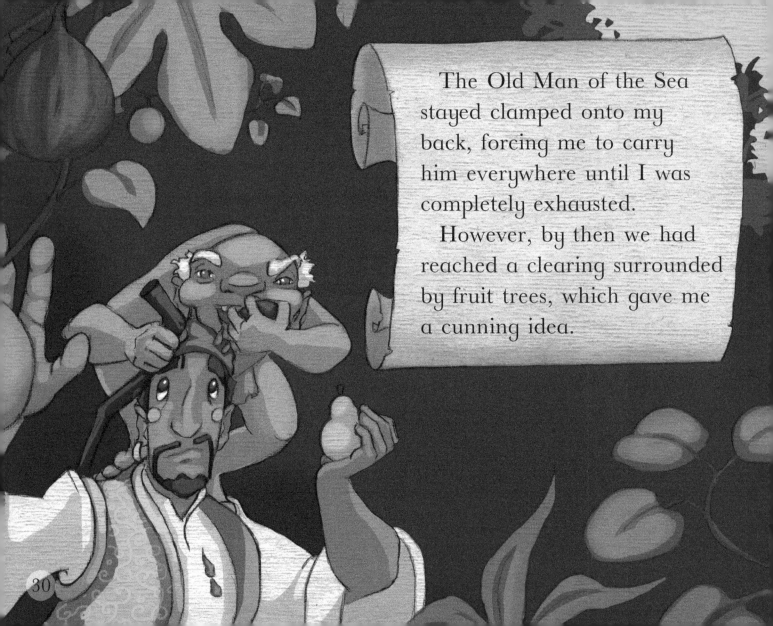

The Old Man of the Sea stayed clamped onto my back, forcing me to carry him everywhere until I was completely exhausted.

However, by then we had reached a clearing surrounded by fruit trees, which gave me a cunning idea.

I started picking the fruit as fast as I could and handing it to the Old Man of the Sea. Just as I expected, he was such a greedy beast that he gulped it all down.

Soon he was so full that he couldn't keep his balance on my shoulders. He started wobbling, giggling and flopping around ...

… until, with a great heave, I flung him right off! Then I went racing back through the forest. And, guess what? As I reached the beach, another ship came passing by.

I waved frantically. The crew saw me and sent a boat out to rescue me.

Phew! By seaweed and gulls' wings – I was safe!